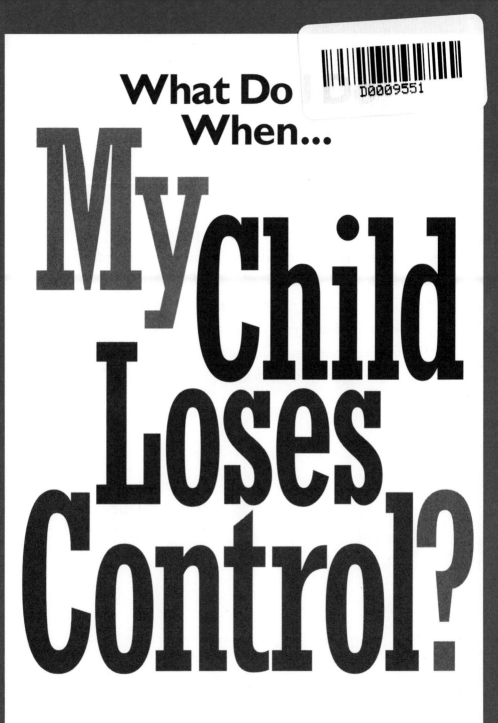

What Do When...

My Child Loses Control?

BY POLLY GREENBERG

DEDICATION

For my daughter Miggie, marvelous mother of two, who thinks it worthwhile to give young children a great deal of guidance in developing self-control. She says, "If you believe that your kid is out of control too often, it might feel better to discuss your worries with a specialist. Together, you can figure out the best thing to do. Teamwork eases most burdens."

Copyright © 1997 by Scholastic Inc.
Illustrations copyright © 1997 by Scholastic Inc.
All rights reserved. Published by Scholastic Inc.
Printed in the U.S.A.
ISBN 0-590-36680-7
7   8   9   10   23   05   06   07

Table of Contents

Introduction

Everybody's child gets out of control now and then. But if it's happening enough to concern you, this book and the others in this series should help.

Child development specialists and effective parents agree that each child needs "quality time" with one or more parent or parenting person every day. "Quality time" is a small block of time — perhaps 15 minutes? — when you:

■ give no directions, instructions, or suggestions of any type whatsoever.

■ offer no criticisms ("No, it goes this way, let me show you").

■ let the child lead 100% of the way in the play, game, activity, or conversation he has chosen.

■ make appreciative or descriptive comments ("That's terrific!" or "You did it!").

Lack of a little leisure time together each day is a leading cause of upset (and upsetting!) behavior in young children. If your child feels deprived of this essential ingredient of good mental health — relaxed, happy time with a loved one — she may signal her distress through frequent bouts of out-of-control behavior.

Out-of-control behavior is behavior that's inappropriate considering the child's age and that neither adult nor child seems able to manage.

Perhaps your child is too persistent — won't quit no matter what you say or do. Or too sensitive — he falls into a funk when his feelings are (too easily!) hurt. Maybe your child is slow to adapt and collapses during daily transitions, or is a master manipulator who tends to tantrum.

A child needs to feel closely and warmly connected to at least one adult who:

■ is in his life for the long term.
■ feels emotionally close and warmly connected to the child.

While not the only cause of behavior problems in children, a common cause is that parents find themselves too busy for their children and feel emotionally uninvolved and distant. This can be the case with parents who are not employed full-time away from home as well as with some who are.

Positive attention (playing a game, taking a walk, reading a story, building, or cooking) creates well-behaved children, and well-behaved children make parents want to give positive attention. So when we work on establishing this circle of happy togetherness, we're indirectly working to improve our child's feeling of well-being, hence behavior. If you've been a too-busy parent, try this with your child most days for six weeks. The more difficult your child, the more prone to episodes of out-of-control behavior, the more important it is to establish a strong, warm friendship.

Evaluate each day, and after your six-week trial period I think you'll notice that your child appreciates and responds positively to your appreciative, responsive, positive approach. Will you give it a whirl?

CHAPTER I

Losing Control:

What Does It Look Like?

When your child loses control, she isn't acting like herself. Losing control can take many forms, but there's a common thread: The child's best self has temporarily been tossed (by uncontrollable anxiety or anger) from the driver's seat. How can you help your child get his most mature self back at the wheel?

When a Child Is Really Out of Control

Lucy was the cutest two-year-old! She was a lovely, kind, busy little person. (And now, she's one of the nicest nine-year-olds you'll ever meet.) But there was a period when horrendous tantrums happened daily on the way home from day care.

No matter what her sensitive mother said or did, she could see storm clouds brewing until Lucy would:

■ suddenly, sullenly hurl herself on the sidewalk, writhing and screaming.

■ thrash, kick, and pummel her mother if, instead of expecting Lucy to walk, her mother carried her, thinking that Lucy might be exhausted after a big day away.

"It was hideous," says Gladys, the mother. She felt:

■ **guilty.**

■ **sorry** for Lucy, who was too little to be so desperately upset.

■ **frustrated** to the nth degree. They were finally together, this was supposed to be cozy time for the two of them.

■ **furious.** Lucy was dominating; Gladys was reacting.

■ **humiliated** to death. People stared at them.

■ **helpless,** absolutely helpless. She tried everything she could think of, but nothing prevented the daily tantrum. Lucy had to go to day care — as a single parent Gladys had to work, and she had to get Lucy home.

The worst thing was that Gladys worried: "Will this pass or is it the way Lucy will **always** be?"

What's a
Parent to Do?

Review relevant facts, later, of course! In the midst of the moment, no doubt you're just trying not to have a tantrum yourself. Consider:

■ your child's **age.**

■ the **setting** — what triggered this tantrum?

■ the **probable source** of these overwhelming emotions. What's been going on in your child's life lately?

Age: Lucy is two, a toddler. We don't expect children younger than three to be able to cope well with a deluge of powerful feelings. Even a child of four or more might collapse occasionally (but not every day!) if stress from some source is too heavy a burden for his small shoulders.

Setting: Lucy's been apart from her mom "forever," or so it feels to her. To your young child, an hour feels like a day. Being separated from family is one of the most stressful things for a small child, even if you've chosen a warm, relaxed setting.

Any child is fatigued at day's end, especially when he's been part of a group and subject to the stimulation, crowding, competition, and accommodation to the needs and schedules of others that group living necessitates.

And transitions often trigger tantrums. Lucy is leaving one world (day care) and entering another (home life).

Probable Source: Six weeks ago, Lucy and her mom moved from another city and all their kin, plus Lucy started day care. Well, all added together, we have our explanation!

What Else Can You Do?

Recognize two types of tantrums: manipulative (see p. 34) and stress-related.

■ **Realize** that your child, under four, is unable to manage a deluge of forceful feelings. His system of self-controls isn't yet fully formed.

He isn't trying to embarrass you, any more than an infant crying because of a bad bellyache is "trying" to wake you, or a big baby who can't quite walk is "trying" to break your back.

■ **Remember!** By four, expect more. From infancy on, teach your child other ways to express feelings than to short circuit. (Words work well! Express your feelings in words, and expect your child to learn the power of language, too.)

When he's calm, teach your tyke that people other than he have feelings and needs. Teach him to care how you feel. But for now (at age two or three and in the throes of a tantrum), your child is unlikely to be very aware of you or of how you feel (embarrassed, angry).

■ **Remain nearby.** A toddler or a two- or three-year-old is terrified by her terrible feelings. She needs to know that a grown-up's in control (She surely isn't!): "I'm here. I'll take care of you. Later, I'll try to help you with your upset feelings."

■ **Refrain** from having a tantrum yourself. When you feel your heart racing, face flushing, and muscles tensing — when you're thinking, "I hate her! I'm gonna hit her!," refrain from raising your voice, using angry postures, expressions, and put-downs.

Your feelings are contagious to your kid. Let her "catch" your calm, not your tantrum.

■ **Reduce** any additional stresses, stimulation, demands, or transitions that you can during your child's high-stress times.

For example, though it might be convenient for Gladys to stop at the supermarket on the way home with Lucy, it would be a bad idea. It would add yet another change of scene, cast of characters, and set of stresses (behavior must be civilized in a store, etc.).

Help Your Child Gain and Maintain Self-Control

Lucy feels disconnected from the extended family she has always lived near and the neighborhood/home she has always lived in. She's not sure who her family is, where her home is.

What Would Help?

■ Arrange visits and/or an audiotape or videotape from loved ones who do, say, sing, and read familiar things. (Get ready, Gladys: Lucy will request it over and over. She'll find it very *soothing*.)

■ Emphasize creating a home, finding a place for everything, and putting everything in its place. Chat about it: Talk about a handful of landmarks of interest to the child in the new neighborhood. The neighbor's birdbath? A McDonald's sign? Try to make Lucy feel connected to the new place. (Lucy will soon realize that she and all her things belong, that she and her mom are family, and that this is their cozy home. She'll feel *secure*.)

■ Help Lucy feel she belongs in the day care. Learn the names of a few children and teachers. Connect with them at least briefly each day. Include their names in pretend play at home. Make and take cupcakes to share. (When Lucy feels included as a member of the club, her *confidence* will rise.)

A child who feels soothed, secure, and confident won't feel or act out of control. (For six more suggestions, see page 21.)

What's Normal?

Encourage Self-Esteem

Here's how to develop your child's self-esteem at each critical stage in his early life.

Birth to 12 Months

Become your baby's best friend. Hold him a lot, and, most important, respond promptly to his needs — for food, change of position, scene, activity, or companionship.

Help him learn to trust and love you. This is the foundation for the strong wish he will have in the future to please you. If your child doesn't care about pleasing you, he will always be out of (your) control.

Twelve to 36 Months

Further develop your friendship with your mobile child. Spend time together. Give her a great deal of encouragement.

Facilitate her independence as she crawls, walks, and climbs. Child-proof her environment. Make appreciative comments, clap, cuddle, avoid being critical or negative.

Three to Seven Years

Continue building bonds between the two of you. Applaud your child's individuality — interests, tastes, temperament. Tolerate quirks — they're probably temporary! Encourage growing competence of many kinds.

Protect your child's "rights" — to not be hurt physically or verbally by adults or children, to speak and play without undue interruption, and to have generous amounts of your time and attention, to sing, look at books, and play together.

Encourage Self-Discipline

Here's how to develop your child's self-discipline:

Birth to 12 Months

After he's three or four months old, watch for the times when your baby tends to tire. Try to get him to sleep at those times every day. Develop a 5-to-10-minute bedtime ritual. Then leave. Have a "no returns" policy except in unusual circumstances. Your baby will learn what's expected and how to put himself to sleep, two important aspects of self-discipline later on.

When you can't tend to him for a few minutes, though he's fussing (perhaps because you're with another child?), say supportive things as he learns to wait. This, too, is self-discipline.

Twelve to 36 Months

You can't child-proof everything — there are still many no-no's. Give a simple, brief explanation. Be firm. "No, Donna. That's Daddy's work." Remove the child. Distraction is a good guidance tool with toddlers. Involve her in something else.

When your toddler is swamped by mad or sad feelings, help her name the feeling, talk about it instead of acting it out, and realize that feelings pass. Learning how to distract oneself, discuss feelings, and have empathy for others are all part of self-discipline. Patiently teach turn-taking and no hurting.

Three to Seven Years

Expect your child to do as you say most of the time. Be friendly and fair, but also firm.

Teach your child of three or more to respect the rights of others (no hurting, interrupting, mean teasing, toy- or turn-grabbing and greediness); to say please, thank you, and excuse me; and to use utensils and not intentionally mess with his food.

Help your three-year-old understand that he can feel any way he wants to, but he's expected to act right. (For how to set sensible limits, see page 18.)

Why Children Lose Control

Two of your child's greatest challenges are to learn:

- *right and wrong.*

- *to control any impulses urging her to act unacceptably.*

A child loses control if she:

- *isn't being firmly guided toward self-discipline.*

- *is so worried or angry that she can't control her impulse to express the stress in an unacceptable way.*

Parenting
Pitfalls

Authoritarian/Coercive Parenting

Coercive parenting can lead to aggressive children, even if "right and wrong" are taught. Is your child sullen, surly, and angry? Does your child often actively defy you and refuse to comply with your requests and rules? Does he threaten, bully, or intimidate other children?

Think about your parenting style and family process. In some families, adults yell, blame, criticize, and command children in an effort to control them. Your child is a copycat. She may learn to yell, blame, criticize, and order people around.

Some children try to influence their parents by being cute. Others try to force their parents to do what they want. When your child is out of control, he forces you to focus on him.

If you know, in your heart of hearts, that this is how things happen in your family, then you (and your partner, if you have one) hold the key to changing your child's out-of-control behavior. For starters, change your way of relating within the family: Talk to your child and treat her as you want her to talk to and treat you, siblings, teachers, and peers.

Children raised coercively may become dangerously docile or deviously dishonest, instead of angrily aggressive.

Negligent/Weak Parenting

Weak parenting can produce out-of-control children, even if the parents are good people. Significant noncompliance, starting in toddlerhood and continuing into the teenage years, correlates with antisocial or delinquent behavior in adolescence.

Besides parents who obviously neglect their children, there are parents who don't take the lead, be the guide, dare to teach, expect, insist. They explain and excuse their child's frequent failures to behave within the range of age-appropriate ways. (Of course, all children fail to behave appropriately occasionally; we're talking about behavior patterns.)

Parents who neglect to expect age-appropriate good behavior (self-control) often have children who are manipulative or lacking in self-esteem.

Regardless of whether your parenting style is too tough or too weak, the long-term results won't be what you're hoping for!

Growing Up Without a Guide

Corinne was one of the most babyish four-year-olds! The problem was that for some unknown reason, Corinne's parents related to her babyish self and seemed not to notice her more capable self.

It would've helped Corinne if her parents had said, whenever needed, "You're a big girl. I don't like so much crying and whining. I like it when we talk together about the interesting things you're doing." A large part of a child's self-esteem comes from being capable.

This applies to Patrick. He howled for half an hour before meals. Then after the meal, because he was hungry, his parents prepared him a complicated snack. His awful behavior was reinforced. If his parents had served him only at mealtimes and told him that he could choose to howl in the bedroom or to behave, he would soon have begun choosing to remain with the family. In the end, he would have been happier.

Children don't like feeling that there's no leader. They need continuing guidance toward becoming independent, competent, and able to manage themselves as their peers and beloved do.

Lack of Fair, Firm
Parenting

T he number one complaint from most parents about their children is that they don't obey, so you know that occasional, mild disobedience is normal. Expect your child to cooperate with you 95% of the time — to do as you say. Direct what you say to the most mature, fair, sensible part of your child's personality.

Your young child is creating in her mind an ideal "self" — a "me as I would like to be." Into this image, she absorbs the judgments of her parents. She swallows what she thinks you think of her, and it mingles with how she'd like to be. If you criticize and correct her a great deal, she may misinterpret what you think of her. As parents we need to send a very clear message: "You're a good person. You're learning good judgment. We all make mistakes sometimes, and we don't always act our best. Children make mistakes. It's our job as your parents to teach you to act right. You're learning to control yourself. You're growing up more all the time."

It's very important for parents to be optimistic in their dealings with each child (even though in our gloomier moments we may not feel all that optimistic!). It's usually quite straightforward: If a child believes that his parents think he's a bad kid, he will be. And, thank goodness, vice versa!

Persist! This Will Work!

If your child is disobeying, then:

1 **Go where your child is.** Get his attention. Politely tell him ONCE, in 10 words or less, exactly what you want him to do.

2 Give no more than one reminder.

3 If necessary, next comes a warning: "If you ..., then ..."

4 Do what you said you would do by way of a mild punishment (a few minutes of time out, miss a favorite video).

5 Whenever he cooperates, smile, pat, or compliment him.

Review pages 12 and 13. Are you doing all these things to strengthen your child's self-esteem and self-discipline every day? If not, better late than never. It's never too late to improve our parenting. I'm still working on it, and my kids are going on 40!

Manage Conflict Constructively

Families that have trouble managing conflict in non-damaging ways tend to have children with more serious behavior problems.

■ **Recognize** anger: Angry faces, voices, stances, words, thoughts.

■ **Manage** anger: Calm down (a five-minute time out for yourself).

■ **Communicate** about solving the problem: Talk respectfully about what each person sees as the problem and his idea for fixing it.

To Spank or Not to Spank?

All child and family professionals advise against spanking because:
• it can easily become abuse.
• it sets the example that might makes right and hitting is okay.
• it deprives children of learning to control their behavior in response to language (your words).

These professionals are <u>not</u> opposed to firm discipline. They 100% recommend it.

Some parents believe that a few smacks on the (fully clothed) bottom from time to time is an important part of their firm discipline. I've never seen any research to support <u>or</u> challenge this idea. We <u>do</u> know that the tell, remind, warn, time-out approach used regularly, works.

Stressful Family Events

Each of us has a mature self and a "childish" (infantile) self. During highly stressful family events, most of us are not able to be our "best" selves consistently. We may act out our extreme feelings of anger or anxiety. This is even more true of young children.

■ **Divorce:** Well-behaved Benny has begun to hurl toys and hurt friends. He clings and cries by day and won't stay in bed at night. Why? His parents have been having bitter fights and nasty tantrums. His parents are absorbed and preoccupied.

■ **Serious Illness/Injury:** Ari was always a spunky, spirited boy who engaged deeply in play, projects, and friendships. Lately, he races wildly around the classroom, can't concentrate, and screams furiously if anyone or anything frustrates him. Why? The word is out: His mother has terminal cancer. Horror haunts his home.

■ **Major Family Changes:** Lucy changes overnight from a calm, centered child to one that is disorganized, highly emotional, and generally unhappy. Why? Her mother moved her to a new home, far from family and everything familiar.

Help Your Child Gain and Maintain Self-Control: Help Him Comprehend Through Conversation and Structure

During the shocking and painful period when his Dad moved out and life changed in many basic ways, Benny's feelings were like those of someone falling from an airplane. Something terrible was happening to him, so quickly that he could hardly comprehend it.

When Ari's mother told the children about her "serious sickness," Ari felt like bolting from a terrifying monster.

When Lucy and her mother moved, Lucy's world became chaotic. Benny, Ari, and Lucy felt and acted out of control.

What would help?

■ A relaxed but regular schedule, with one event following the other in a very routine way. (These children will begin to feel *competent* — they will know how to live their new lives.)

■ Fair but firm rules to serve as standards, guidelines, and "fences." (This will help children feel *safe,* especially from their frightening feelings.)

■ Brief but accurate explanations and conversations to help Benny, Ari, and Lucy understand what's going on. (The children will be *calmed* by reasonable rules and simple explanations.)

A child who feels competent, safe, and calm is not likely to feel or act out of control. If your child is frequently out of control, do everything you can to help him feel included and connected to his family and extended family and friends.

Help him understand what's going on in his life with sensible routines and rules and conversation explaining them. (For three more suggestions, see page 11.)

Tips for Supporting Your Child

1 Help him acknowledge and express concerns, fears, guilt, jealousy, feelings of rejection, isolation, and anger through conversation, play, art, and vigorous exercise.

2 Offer accurate information, but little by little. Let your child get used to this, one step at a time. She doesn't need to know all possible eventual scenarios, or the worst, at first.

3 Often comment on things that remain the same and have fun!

An Overprogrammed Life

If your child is often out of control, the best cure could be more parental care. Think of young children's lives a generation or two ago. They didn't have to hurry here, hustle there, rush from lesson to lesson and from sitter to school to sitter. Could your child use less pressure and more of your presence? Nonintrusive supervision goes a long way in preventing behavior problems. Being in the room helps.

■ **Guilty Grown-ups:** Sometimes, we as parents are overprogrammed, and truth to tell we know we're overprogramming our children because of a sneaking suspicion that we're ignoring them. We can help our kids more by finding child-care programs (preferably NAEYC-accredited) with well-credentialed staff and schools with lively (rather than predominantly sit-down) programs than by spoiling them when we're with them. By "spoiling," I mean allowing them to act like rotten people.

■ **Holidays:** Family togetherness and traditions are very good for children, even though they get excited and perhaps exhibit less-than-perfect control. (If your child was born with an excitable temperament and his daily life is overstimulating, holidays can be rough.) If your family travels and/or if lots of relatives are involved, your child may become overwhelmed, hence out of control. Consider what you can do to keep the fun parts, and pare down the parts that don't work.

■ **Birthdays:** Some parents in modern-day, materialistic America give their children most of what they want but little of what they need. More than a million more toys, your child needs quiet time with you to do something he likes to do.

Think of Your Child as an Iceberg

If your child is:

1 extremely aggressive with other children (significantly more than other children of the same age — observe!),

2 usually rejected by peers (don't be the queen of denial), or

3 constantly in a victim position (according to him, it's always someone else's fault),

then something is not "average" or "typical." If your child disobeys, whines, cries much more than mildly and briefly once a day, or frequently seems confused, something isn't quite right.

You've probably heard it said that behavior is "just the tip of the iceberg." Only a small piece of an iceberg is visible. Most of it is submerged below the dark waters. As you try to understand out-of-control behavior in your child, you may find it useful to think about what could be going on beneath the surface.

Any of the following things can influence a child's behavior, and any combination or accumulation of them can make matters much worse:

■ Low self-esteem (promote skills, interests, and competencies),

■ Parental expectations for behavior-related "follow-up" discipline that are too high and severe (ease up!) or too low and ineffective (get tough!),

■ Stressful life events (birth or death of a family member, job loss, inappropriate child-care setting or school),

■ Undiagnosed learning disability or neurological problems, such as a high lead level.

Any clues here that you might want to investigate?

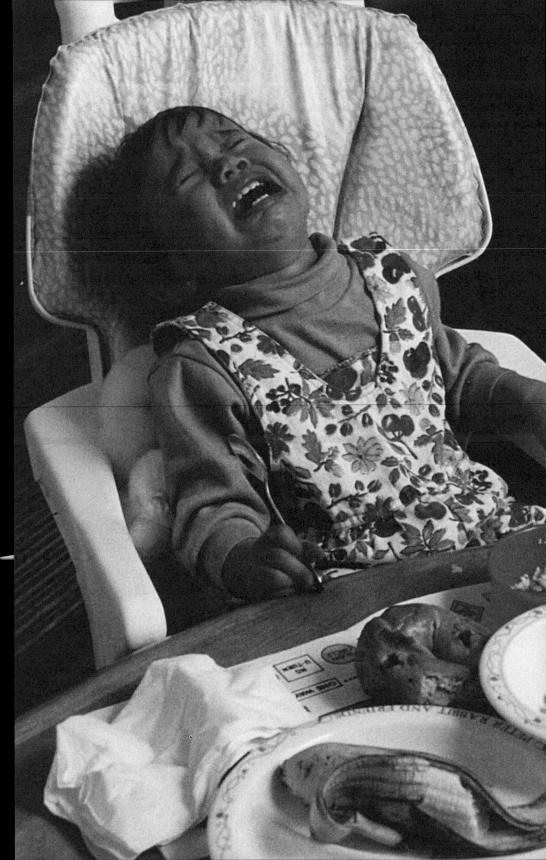

CHAPTER III

When Do Children Lose Control?

Fatigue, feeling unwell, and frustration cause little kids to lose it.

Transitions are tough. Does your child dawdle or wheel and deal when you declare it time to brush teeth, get dressed, or go somewhere? Some kids' reaction to anything new is to reject it — and throw a fit if a parent pushes.

Helpful hints follow!

STOCK BOSTON

When Children Lose Control
...at Home

Plan! Prevent as many frustrations for your child (thus yourself!) as possible. Many will remain: Life's like that. It's important for children to learn to cope with a moderate amount of frustration — to manage anger in acceptable ways. Here are some tips for preventing most blowups ...

... When Brushing:

■ Have a routine. Brushing follows the meal, a story follows the teeth.

■ Offer choices. Buy three brush colors, types of tubes, flavors (it costs the same in the end).

■ Reward each perfect week. Let your child choose from a decorated shoebox of party favors and cheapo treasures.

■ Acknowledge feelings — it's boring, no comprehensible reason, interrupts your busy child.

... at Mealtime:

■ Develop the habit of serving ONLY three meals and three healthy snacks a day. Hungry children eat.

■ Know that children are messy eaters. Throwing food, excessive messing, and playful pouring are "statements" that the child is ready to wash up and go play.

■ Model curiosity about new foods and taking pleasure in variety, but realize that most children prefer the same old same old and react negatively to new foods.

■ Teach manners. Your child can have a happy meal with you for company before the family eats, or he can behave reasonably and eat with the family.

... When Dressing

Here are 12 tips for surviving:

1 **Don't buy** tight necks, complicated fasteners, scratchy fabrics, or socks in more than one color.

2 **Store out-of-season clothes.** Avoid the jacket-in-July, swimsuit-in-January battle.

3 **Sort and label:** Use hangers of four colors (four drawers, four shelves) for school, play, dress-up, and special clothes.

4 **Limit "big" choices:** Pin complete outfits together: "Will you choose this outfit or the other?" Praise decision making.

5 **Offer small choices:** "Want to wear your wolf belt?" "Which hair ribbons? None today? Okay."

6 **Tolerate your child's declaration of individuality and independence.** Ignore small sartorial peculiarities, but don't let her leave home looking weird.

7 **Teach taste:** Compliment pleasing color combinations.

8 **Reduce distractions:** Decide on a "dressing room" — a boring room (the bathroom?) with no other kids, TV off, blinds shut.

9 **Allow tons of time!**

10 **Make silly jokes:** Put the pants on her head. Laugh (lovingly) about your task-orientedness and your child's pokiness.

11 **Let the thermometer and clock be the boss.** Mount an easy-to-read thermometer outside a window, and keep a clock handy. Let your child see for himself.

12 **Brace yourself** for "I can't do it," or "Let me do it myself," or, if your child is two, both at the same time, accompanied by shrieks and howls.

When Children Lose Control
...Out in the World

Plan appropriately, and expect children to behave on an outing.

■ Be sure everyone is rested (has napped, if your child is still a napper), fed, and quenched (unless you're going to a family restaurant — then be sure they're hungry) and not engrossed in an activity that will be interrupted.

■ Tell your child the plan — five minutes ahead if she's three or less, a little more in advance if he's four or more. (Time to prepare oneself is always nice, don't you think?)

■ Make it a short shop, fast eat, or quick trip to the museum. The goal: At the end of the outing, the kids and adults are all still smiling.

... With an Audience

Why do children seem to lose control more often if there is an audience? When you and your child are shopping? On the bus? On playdates? While visiting relatives?

As we've said, some children find new, "seldom seen," or frequently changing situations or transitions from one scenario to another stressful. They make a scene because they're short-circuiting. If your child is slow to adapt, focus on making treacherous transitions and outings tranquil:

■ "I think you're cranking because you didn't get to finish ..." (Allow time for your child to finish what he's doing.)

■ "Grandpa, Jenny's going to sit on my lap for a few minutes, then it might be your turn." (Smile, wink, give Jenny time to adjust.)

Some children misbehave (in general, as well as in public) because they feel inadequate. Is your child innately shy or socially awkward? Maybe she feels she doesn't know how to perform all the social niceties you expect. Coach her, break it down, and teach each teeny piece.

"While we're in the store you can walk by yourself near me, hold my hand, or ride in the shopping cart (stroller). If someone talks to you, you can talk to them or you can just look at them and smile."

Some children misbehave to get revenge or power over you. Don't allow your child to win — if she does, she'll know she has found a great weapon and will use it against you again!

Act cool! Do what you would do if there were no audience: State what you expect, remind, warn (once), and do it.

The warning might be "If you aren't friendly to Aunt Annie, you will not have any treats in your lunch box all week."

Or, "If you don't cooperate with me now and play properly with Paul, I'm not going to cooperate with you later and take you to the park. Your choice."

You probably won't notice it at the time, but rest assured: Parents who tough it out when their kids lose control in public, remaining calm, loving, and <u>firm</u>, win admiring glances from those around them!

Shopping With Your Child?

1 Offer a choice of fruit treats as you arrive — choosing and eating will distract for a while. See page 18 for basic ways to discipline anyplace you go.

2 Don't rush your child. Stop to smell the oranges.

3 Or splurge — use a sitter and enjoy yourself — it's easier than a scene.

How Children

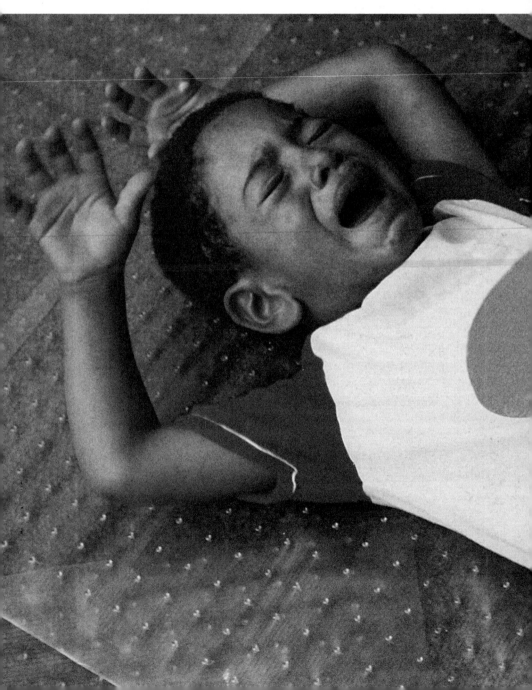

Lose Control

Children fall apart, strike out, and find other ways to demonstrate power, seek attention, or signal hidden problems. Whatever form the uproar takes, the cure involves:

- *getting your behavior under control.*

- *spending lots of leisurely time with her.*

- *supporting him with firm, fair discipline.*

- *solving stressful problems in the family.*

- *seeking professional help when you need it.*

Out of Control With Other Kids?

There's a well-established link between serious behavior problems in a child — frequent out-of-control behavior — and social problems. Children will dislike your child and won't play with her if she's too often out of line. So when you patiently teach your child how to get along with you, siblings, and everyone else, you're increasing her chances of developing friendships with peers. Not actively teaching social behavior to children is mean to them — it hurts their chances for a happy life.

Hitting, Throwing, Biting

Teach your child:

- "Hurting (wrecking things) isn't allowed. I won't allow anyone to hurt anyone."

- "First, let's take 10 big breaths and cool off. Then we can talk."

- "Use words." (Help the children do this.)

- "Look at each other, listen to each other, take turns explaining what you want once each." (Stand by, remind, assist.)

- "How can we solve the problem? Can you each suggest a good idea?"

- "Okay, those are good ideas. Now what's the plan?" (Stick around until the children are working it out.)

- "You kids solved that problem really well!"

  If you've gone through this process with this child already

today and are feeling that enough is enough, use time out:

- "If you can't manage your behavior just now, you can play (by yourself, somewhere else) until you feel more cooperative."

What's normal? Some three- and four-year-olds (not all) physically act out angry or disruptive impulses (hit, knock down a block structure) as often as once every few weeks. If it's a child's pattern to assault or purposefully disturb others more often than this, or if your child is more than four, focus on changing the extreme behavior. Biting, for example, cannot be tolerated in a child above toddlerhood — stand close, don't let it happen.

Extreme Patience and Constant Coaching Can Help This Child

Occasionally we see a child who "just doesn't get it" socially. His social skills are strikingly poor. He misses obvious social cues. He can't see what everyone else — including children his age — sees easily. (I'm busy, you're exasperating me. I'm getting angry.) Other children reject him because he behaves so inappropriately and is so out of it. Children and adults alike consider the child weird. Is your child like this?

A child like this may seem hyper, or like a leech, and can drive parents and teachers crazy. But he's lonely, and usually depressed, because he lacks the ability to connect interpersonally and is starving for the warmth and comfort of friendship. You and your child's teacher can work closely, with this information in mind, to help him succeed socially. His out-of-control behavior will then significantly improve.

Tantrums and Tantrum Tamers

Sam says, "Our five-year-old goes into uncontrollable rages at least several times a week. Some small frustration sets him off. We try to reason with him and meet his needs, but nothing works. Eventually, his tantrums tire him, taper off, and end in tears. Is this normal?"

What is normal? Sam just put his finger on a problem that causes many parents extra hassle and anxiety. How do you know which behaviors are in the normal range and which are "off the chart"? Thinking about whether such frequent tantrums are normal (for a five-year-old — this is not a two-year-old) is a great place to start thinking about what to do.

Is your child 3 or more?

If so, tantrums are definitely *not* the norm and your child needs to learn age-appropriate ways to cope. Do everything discussed on pages 8-11, modified as needed to suit your situation.

Temper tantrums and time out

If a child of four or more years of age has a raging tantrum and there are no extraordinary circumstances (fever, parents just had a shrieking fight), he isn't "acting his age." You don't have to spend time with him trying to "understand," while he flails and wails. Wait till he gets himself under control. Even then, you may think it best just to drop it.

Use time out. "Time out!" Sam says, in dismay. "How could I do that? He kicks and crashes. He wouldn't go! He *might* go, but he would keep coming back. What if he's still thrashing around when the time out is up? What if he wrecks the room?"

Here are some ideas that work for many parents.

If your child won't go to an out-of-the-way time-out place:

1 Use reverse time out.

Walk out yourself. Shut yourself in a room where you have a good magazine to read, and enjoy it. Keep one there, just in case. (If necessary, take the baby, but it's better to leave your other children out of this, if possible.) After the storm has subsided and blue skies appear again, say nothing about the wild behavior. Move on in a friendly way.

2 Start time out after the tantrum has wound down.

Say, "You'll start your time out when you're enough in control of yourself to go into your room." Later, say, "I see you've gotten yourself calm. Good. Now spend some time alone (as many minutes as equal the child's age), and figure out what to do next time you feel frustrated instead of having a fit. I'll give you the timer. Come back in x minutes if you feel ready."

3 If this causes junior to renew his tantrum, go through the same procedures again.

Don't discuss anything with your child. Don't reward this unacceptable behavior with your attention. (Is there anything a child considers more rewarding?) State what is now going to happen and make it happen.

4 Give a choice: time out or the loss of something he likes.

(The video he usually gets to watch one afternoon a week? The pack of sugar-free gum he gets on Saturdays?) If your child weighs almost as much as you do, or you have a bad back or some such, say, "You can go to time out right now or you can skip the video, your choice."

If your child won't stay in the time-out place:

Your child of four years or more must learn to do as you say. Say, "If you can't make yourself stay where I told you to stay, the door will be locked. If you can manage yourself and tell yourself to stay there, the door can stay open. Your choice."

Many children will stay where you put them (in a boring corner, on the sofa with everyone out of the room, in their room, in any unoccupied room). Others keep yoyoing back to you, sobbing and screaming.

Most enraged jack-in-the-box children quickly learn to stay put because they see that you mean it, and they definitely prefer that the door be open. If yours is a highly excitable, strong-willed child, you'll probably have to lock him in. So do — but only until he has quieted.

If your child still resembles a tornado when the timer indicates that the time out should end:

Remind him once that he can return when he has gotten himself under control. He can return any time he can be "regular Ronnie."

But what if your child threatens to wreck any room you put him in for a time out?

Most children don't make this threat, and even among those who do threaten, most don't actually do it. Nonetheless, it's best to be prepared for a possible room trasher. Plan ahead. Decide on a room that doesn't have your collection of precious porcelain cows in it, and "baby-proof" it. Remove anything dangerous of course — crayons and markers or whatever else your child might use to ruin the walls, etc. If he dumps all the drawers, yanks all the bedding off the bed, and pulls down the curtains, say nothing and do nothing. During the next few weeks, he'll have to find his toys, his clothes, and a place to sleep as the need arises.

What if you're in public?

Do exactly what you would do if no one was present, regardless of how embarrassed you are — don't let your child manipulate you! Tell the child loudly that he will not be invited next time. Keep your word.

What should you expect and work toward?

As children reach two, three, four years of age, they need to learn (we need to teach) a variety of essential social skills, such as how to:

■ distinguish between **feelings** (okay to have) and **acts** (we can't act out everything we feel).

■ share materials, activities, and the attention of a friendly adult.

■ compete and cooperate.

■ argue and settle arguments.

■ negotiate and compromise.

It takes time for young children to learn all this, but in each situation the child's grown-ups should firmly guide her toward the goal.

When a little child is flooded by strong emotions, he can't listen to anyone. He can't accept advice or constructive criticism. He can't participate in conversation. Sometimes he can get his feelings under control if his parents release some of the pressure with a sentence indicating understanding. If this doesn't prevent a tantrum, don't engage further.

Why would a child act like this?

Most likely, he's had previous experience leading him to believe that he can force his parents to back down. He thinks he can intimidate and overpower them. Letting a child continue to get away with this is courting disaster. Just wait till he's a teenager!

CHAPTER V

Out of Control

at School?

Parents know their individual child best, but experienced teachers know what's typical for children this age.
If you're worried about your child's behavior, then visit her classroom regularly and talk often with her teacher.
Share and compare.

When a Teacher Says There's a Problem...

During a fall conference, Carl's kindergarten teacher told Karen, his mother, that Carl is "hyper," and "probably is an ADHD child" (Attention Deficit Hyperactive Disorder). She said, "He might benefit from Ritalin" (a controversial drug sometimes prescribed for children who have ADHD).

Karen was distressed. Yes, she has been having "discipline problems" with her feisty five-year-old son. He has been behaving "beyond the bounds — on the wild side" (as Karen describes his behavior) frequently and dramatically since school started.

Karen sees Carl as a spirited child, a lively child, an ever-so-active and busy child. But does he need a scary "label"? Does he need drugs?

The teacher told Karen that Carl fidgets and squirms in his seat, talks when he shouldn't (forgets to raise his hand and to wait for a talking turn), makes careless mistakes on his worksheets because he doesn't pay attention to details, and is easily distracted.

"I believe you," Karen said to the teacher. "But is this a *disease*? A *disorder*? Or a normal, active young child?"

Karen asks her sister, a well-trained preschool teacher, what *she* thinks. Her sister says, "Maybe he needs a more project-oriented curriculum with more outdoor play, big block play, musical activities, and time to make friends."

Karen Should Consider:

1 Is a teacher qualified and credentialed to make a medical diagnosis?

No, never. A teacher should describe the behaviors that concern her and ask the parents (*both* parents, if possible) if they:

- see these behaviors at home (occasionally? often?)

- have heard about these problems before (from other teachers? relatives? playmates' parents? sitters? occasionally? often?)

- would please spend time in the classroom comparing their child's behavior to that of other children.

2 Am I, as a parent, listening carefully to what the teacher is saying about my child, even though it's upsetting?

Parents should gather and honestly think over information about their child's behavior in the ways just mentioned. There *must* be a reason for the teacher's concern. Then parents can compare their observations against what else they know about their child and decide what to do.

3 Is this program (preschool, day care, kindergarten, primary class) appropriate for a child this age (whatever age your child is), and for my child, specifically?

National standards explain the best classroom climate for child development and the best way to educate young children. Karen and other parents may want to:

- ask for "position statements" (easy-to-read, explicit descriptions of opinions or standards) and other materials from relevant professional associations.

- read professional publications, available at many libraries and schools.

It could be that the *program's* problems are bigger than the *kid's*. And it could be that your child needs help getting his behavior under control.

CHAPTER VI

When Life Is a

Chronic Crisis

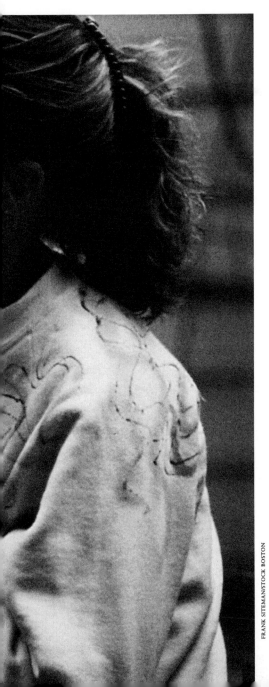

You have all the clues you need to know that something is wrong, and your family needs help. Have you read good books and magazines about parenting? Can you take some parenting classes? Much is known about effective, happier childrearing. Help is out there if you want to go after it.

What You Don't Know
Might Hurt You —

T here are some neurobiological reasons for problems pertaining to social understanding, impulse control, sudden rages, and unusual aggressiveness, but even so, effective parenting is essential, and in most of our children, there are no exceptional neurological causes for tantrums. We can help our children overcome.

If you're unsure about how severe your child's or family's problems are, it would be good to consult a licensed mental health professional (*child* psychiatrist, clinical *child* psychologist, *child* psychoanalyst, or psychiatric social worker specializing in children) who is experienced in working with children who consistently exhibit extremely difficult behaviors.

Beware! There are ill-trained people out there. Be certain that the professional you select is licensed.

Also, there are nearly 100 different specializations in the mental health field. You need a person trained and experienced in working with children who act like your child acts.

A wise adult consults an accountant, lawyer, doctor, or child development professional when the need arises — no need to be ashamed of consulting a professional when it concerns probably the most important part of your life — your child!

If your child is functioning within the wide range of what we consider "normal," although, at the moment, his behavior is at the far border of okay — too often out of control — the understandings and suggestions in this little book can help you:

■ promote your child's healthy development.

- prevent problems from setting like cement or worsening.

- considerably improve the not-so-hot stuff that's going on.

- enjoy your child a whole lot more.

If You Have Serious Doubts, See a Specialist

Even in extreme cases in which a child psychiatrist (an M.D. who specializes in mind/body problems in children) has carefully examined the child and given a diagnosis, the insights and techniques offered here (if put into practice regularly) will reduce the level of your child's behavior problems and will result in relief for your whole family.

Speaking of the whole family, fostering friendships between each member and each *other* member — focusing on strengthening each segment of a friendship web within your family — is worth the time it takes.

What does each pair of people like to do together? Bake? Play simple board games? Hike? Make music? Roughhouse?

Do you know the children's song that goes "The More We Get Together, the Happier We'll Be"? Not bad advice for busy families with or without an out-of-control child!

You Need to Lead

From the moment a baby is born, she's a physically separate entity who initiates lots of behavior (such as crying, oh, woe is me!). Surprise: You do not fully control how your baby behaves. (If you try to be totally in control, both you and the baby will be totally frustrated).

Your children move through the toddler stage of becoming more psychologically separate, more independent. They crawl away, walk and run in many directions, and often think independently, too. No doubt this is not news to you: Your child doesn't always think, choose, and do what you think she should. You don't fully control what your toddler or two-year-old decides to do. (You can provide fair, firm guidance, yet your toddler will occasionally "get into things," balk like a burro, become enraged, and in other ways misbehave. Parents just have to put up with some of this — it's part of the package.)

When your child is three, four, and five years old, expert parents and child development specialists expect him to be less headstrong and more reasonable. Still, he'll have many ideas and will make many behavioral choices that you may not agree with, approve of, or control.

BUT — and this is a BIG but — blaming a young child for having big-time behavior problems just won't cut the mustard.

Although your child contributes her own temperament, point of view, and problems to your relationship, the parent is the person in the best position to guide the child's

■ character development,

- personality characteristics, and

- general behavior.

The parent (or parenting person, perhaps the grandmother) is in the best position to shape the nature of the relationship because an adult is more mature, wise, and powerful than a young child.

Pam felt she was almost at the point of no return: "My six-year-old son's manipulativeness was a pattern." Pam saw that it was now or never, to stop the constant wheeling and dealing.

"I assumed Bobby was out-of-control because there's no father. Suddenly, I see that although it's sad he doesn't have a dad, he's disobedient mainly because I've <u>allowed</u> it. Now his choice is to comply by my second request, or be denied something he likes. No discussion. That's enough power for a child." Right on, Pam!

It's often said that parenting is like dancing — the parent leads, the child "follows," and together the partners create the dance.

If you're having problems with your child:

- **First** change your behavior.

- **Then** guide your child toward the behaviors that you believe are appropriate.

If you're having problems with your child, the bad news is that you will have to work hard to make things better. The good news is that, as the parent, you are in the ideal position to influence your child in the right direction.

Endnote

You want your child to change, but are you ready to change? Many parents have good intentions about doing things differently. But the hard part is changing our own behavior and solving the problems in our lives so that our children can respond to us better emotionally, therefore behaviorally. Here's a chance to prove that you can be flexible — if one approach isn't working, will you try another? Show you can grow!

Young children think differently than adults do. Therefore, they easily misunderstand. But your child *feels* in the same way that you or anyone else does: If there is anger in the air, or contempt, worry, or stress in your voice, your child feels it. That's why it's particularly important that parents deal with their personal or marital issues (with outside help if needed), or these issues are guaranteed to become roadblocks between the child and potential behavioral change.

Parents are teachers. You are the teacher your child wants to please more than any other teacher in the whole wide world. Teach your child what you expect. If she "forgets," remind her once. Warn her once about the consequence if she doesn't cooperate. Be sure that the consequence can be carried out.

Take heart! If your child often acts in unacceptable ways — is out of control — remember that he somehow learned to act that way. Backtrack. Play detective. Analyze. What "taught" him that he could get away with this behavior? If your child learned to act unacceptably, he can also learn to act acceptably. Our job as parents is to help each of our children learn to be a good person. A happier child and family will be your well-earned reward!